Make Your Own Toys and Games

D0275656

This Armada book belongs to:

_____

_____

_____

Make Your Own Toys and Games

HAL DANBY

Illustrated by Brian Wilson

An Armada Original

Make Your Own Toys and Games was first published
in 1979 in the U.K. in Armada by Fontana Paperbacks,
14 St James's Place, London SW1A 1PF.

© Hal Danby & Marion Lloyd 1979

Printed in Great Britain by
William Collins Sons & Co. Ltd.,
London and Glasgow

Contents

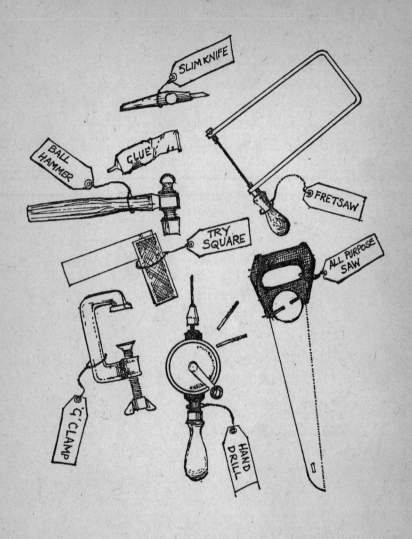

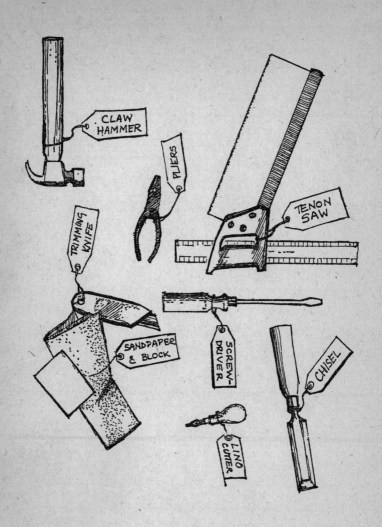

Introduction

The toys and games described in this book vary in difficulty and cost. Most of them can be made from materials which are likely to be found about the house.

It has been assumed that most households have a simple selection of small tools, but if, occasionally, a special tool is required, it is listed at the head of the page.

WARNING
PAINT CAN BE DANGEROUS

Most household paint contains poisonous lead. This type of paint, even when dry, can be dangerous – or even fatal – if eaten or sucked by a small child.

Please, where possible, use lead-free enamels which can be bought from craft or model shops. The Humbrol or Joy ranges are ideal.

For Best Results...

CUTTING

ALWAYS:

Use a really sharp knife (it's safer than a blunt one).

Cut along a straight edge where possible (e.g. a metal-edged ruler).

NEVER:

Put your fingers in front of the blade.

Cut anything which is not held securely.

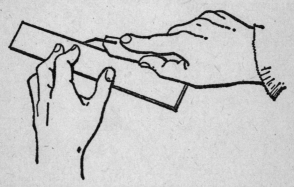

SAWING

ALWAYS:

Use the right saw for the job.

Mark your wood with ruled lines before sawing straight cuts – and saw just to one side of the line.

Avoid splitting wood by going carefully towards the end of a cut.

NEVER:

Use a blunt or broken saw.

Saw wood which is not securely held.

How to saw cubes accurately:

To saw a length of square wood at an exact right angle, draw pencil lines at right angles across two adjacent surfaces, using a trysquare.

Hold the wood in a clamp or vice so that you can see both ruled lines at once while working. Starting at the point where the lines meet, saw through the piece of wood from corner to corner.

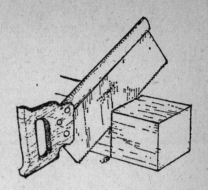

GLUEING

ALWAYS:

Follow instructions carefully.

Hold glued articles together where possible with clamps, weights, rubber bands, etc.

Wait for glue to dry completely.

NEVER:

Apply glue to dirty surfaces.

NAILING

ALWAYS:

Use the right nails for the job.

Rule a line for the nails when working along an edge.

NEVER:

Use rusty or crooked nails.

Spoil the wood with hammer marks.

Use a large nail near an edge. This could split the wood.

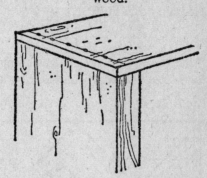

PAINTING

ALWAYS:

Paint bare wood with wood primer first.

Sandpaper wood smooth beforehand.

Fill wood cracks with plaster filler.

Stir paint thoroughly.

Use undercoat before the gloss coat.

Wait until one coat is completely dry before applying the next.

Clean your brushes very thoroughly.

NEVER:

Paint on to a dirty surface.

Apply too much paint at a time.

Magic Square

YOU WILL NEED
A square of thick card
Poster paints

SPECIAL EQUIPMENT
None

Copy the pattern illustrated on to the card, and cut out the shapes using a sharp knife. Paint the pieces with different colours, on both sides.

Jumble all the pieces, and ask a friend to put them back together to make a square. It's not as easy as it looks ...

Instant Whizzer

YOU WILL NEED
*The lid from a coffee jar – or a
   very big button
Thin string or strong thread
A nail
Enamel paints*

SPECIAL EQUIPMENT
None

1 Make two holes in the
   centre of the lid by banging
   the nail through it into a
   block of wood.

2 Paint the lid with enamel
   paints in a spiral pattern.

3 Thread a long piece of
   string through the holes and
   knot the ends. Twirl the lid
   round and round – and pull
   the string taut to make it
   whizz, first one way, then
   the other, for as long as you
   can.

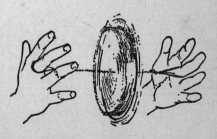

Bongo Drums

YOU WILL NEED
2 *empty paint tins without lids,*
   one large and one small
Sheet of very good quality
   cartridge paper
Brown paper tape
Decorative wallpaper
Wallpaper paste
Plastic electrical insulating
   tape

SPECIAL EQUIPMENT
None

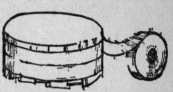

1 Cover the tops of the tins with the cartridge paper and tape it on as tightly as possible all the way round, with brown paper tape. Dampen the surface of the paper with a sponge and put the tins in the airing cupboard, or other warm place, to dry. The paper will shrink and give you a tight drumskin.

2 Cut out pieces of wallpaper and paste them round the sides of the tins, as shown, using wallpaper paste. Cut out circles of wallpaper and paste them on the bottom of the tins.

3 Tape the two drums tightly together with the plastic tape stuck round the tins three times at the top and bottom.

Hold the bongo drums between your knees and play them very fast with the tips of your fingers.

Shove Twopenny

YOU WILL NEED
*Good quality plywood, 10 mm
  thick
36cm length of 25 mm square
  wood
Blackboard paint
Varnish
Wood glue
Wood screws
Masking tape*

SPECIAL EQUIPMENT
Ruler with metal edge

1 Cut out a piece of plywood to the measurements shown. Cut two 28cm lengths of 25 mm square wood. Sandpaper all edges and surfaces smooth.

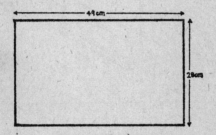

2 Glue and screw the wood across the top and bottom of the board as shown. One piece must be 8 cm from one end of the board.

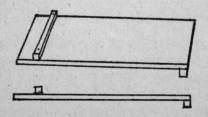

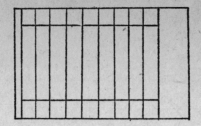

3 Rule a grid of 9 lines across the board, 32 mm apart, 10 cm from the front edge. Rule a line down either side of the board, 4 cm from the edge.

4 With a sharp nail or pointed instrument held against a metal-edged ruler, score deep lines along all the ruled lines.

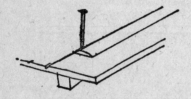

5 Fill the lines across with black paint, then sandpaper the board completely smooth until the paint remains only in the scored lines.

6 Give the board several coats of varnish, sandpapering it very lightly in between each coat. When it is completely dry, stick masking tape along the downward lines, and paint the outside edges of the board with blackboard paint. Don't remove the tape until the paint is completely dry.

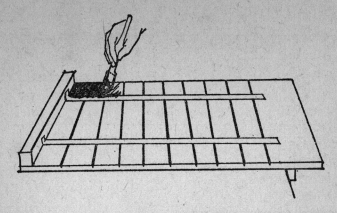

7 Collect six twopenny pieces, and a piece of chalk with which to mark the score on the board, and you're ready to play.

Cork It Up

YOU WILL NEED
Scraps of plywood
Stick-on baize
Wood glue
Sandpaper
Panel pins
Lettraset numbers
10 *corks*
Emulsion and enamel paints
Varnish
2 *dice*

SPECIAL EQUIPMENT
A drill with a 15 mm bit

1 Cut out six pieces of plywood to the measurements shown.

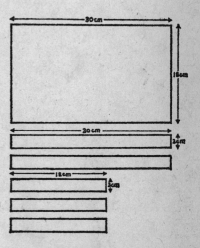

2 Make a shallow box, with panel pins and glue, using five of the pieces. Paint the outside of the box with two coats of emulsion and then with a gloss finish.

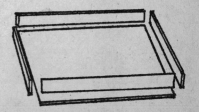

3 Cut a block of wood to the measurements shown. Drill ten holes through it, 15 mm in diameter and 5 mm apart. Sandpaper it smooth.

4 Paint the block with two coats of emulsion. When dry, stick Lettraset figures below the holes, numbering them from 1 to 10. Give the block a coat of varnish to protect the numbers.

5 Glue the block into the box. Trim one end of the sixth piece of wood so that it fits across the inside of the box, sandpaper it smooth, and glue it alongside the holed piece, to make a partition, as shown.

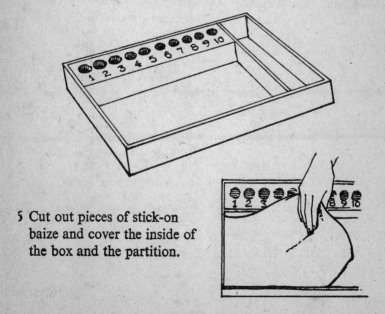

5 Cut out pieces of stick-on baize and cover the inside of the box and the partition.

7 Collect ten corks and make
sure they will all fit into the
drilled holes. You may have
to trim them slightly.
Paint them with enamel
paints to match the outside
of the box. Keep them in
the partitioned-off section
of the box.

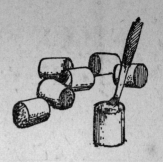

How to play "Cork It Up": Two or more players can play.
Each player throws two dice into the box – and continues to
throw until he has finished his turn. The object of the game
is to cork up all the numbered holes, using the total score
shown on the dice at each throw. For instance, if your first
throw gives you a total of 8, you can cork up holes 1 and 7,
or 2 and 6, or 3 and 5, or 8. Throw again to cork up more
holes, and keep throwing until either all the holes are corked,
or you are left with no holes that correspond with the score
thrown.

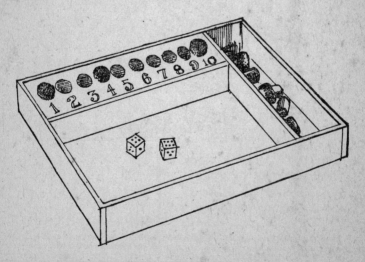

Playground Cricket Stumps

YOU WILL NEED
3 60 cm (24") lengths of
   broomstick or 25 mm (1")
   dowelling
Scrap of wood
12 mm ($\frac{1}{2}$") dowelling
Wood glue
Sandpaper

SPECIAL EQUIPMENT
Drill with a 25 mm bit
Round file

1 With a round file, make
semi-circular indentations
across one end of each of
the lengths of broomstick.

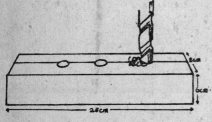

2 Cut a piece of wood to the
measurements shown for the
base of the stumps. Rule a
line down the centre of the
wood and drill three holes
along the line, an inch apart,
through the wood.

3 Glue the lengths of broomstick into place, making
sure that the indentations
across the tops are aligned
so that they run in a
straight line.

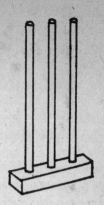

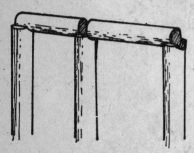

4 Cut a short length of
dowelling in half for the
bails.

The Four-sided Coin

YOU WILL NEED
Small piece of thick (2 mm) card
Drawing materials

SPECIAL EQUIPMENT
A sharp knife

By revolving this "magic" coin between your thumb and fore-finger, you can make it appear to have four different faces.

1 Cut out a circle of card approximately 5 cm (2″) in diameter. Copy the face illustrated on to one side. (This will make the first and third faces of the coin.)

2 Turn the card over and draw the second and fourth faces – as shown – *crossways* to the faces on the other side.

Practise twirling and turning the coin between your fingers so that you show the four faces in turn – and invent a running commentary to accompany the trick to make it even more effective.

1st. and 3rd.

2nd. and 4th.

Glider

YOU WILL NEED

A balsa wood offcut approximately 45 cm × 18 mm × 6 mm
Scraps of 2 mm balsa
Sandpaper
Dressmaking pins
Balsa cement
Lead or nails

SPECIAL EQUIPMENT

None

1 To make the fuselage, cut the balsa approximately 10 cm from one end to make a sloping surface about 8 cm long, as shown. Cut the balsa away from the bottom of the slope to the rear end. Round off the nose and smooth all surfaces with sandpaper.

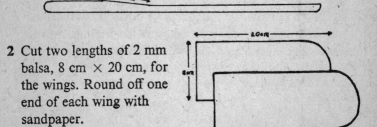

2 Cut two lengths of 2 mm balsa, 8 cm × 20 cm, for the wings. Round off one end of each wing with sandpaper.

3 With the fuselage lying on a flat surface, glue on the wings accurately, at an upward angle, as shown. The front of each wingtip should be 30 mm from the ground. Put an extra fillet of glue between the underside of the wings and the fuselage. Fix the wings in place with pins until the glue is completely dry.

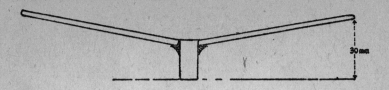

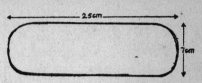

4 Cut a piece of 2 mm balsa, 7 cm × 25 cm, for the tail. Round off the ends with sandpaper.

5 Cut a piece of 2 mm balsa, 7 cm × 8 cm to make the tail fin. Round off one corner.

6 Glue the tail fin on to the larger tail piece, then glue the whole tail on to the fuselage.

7 The glider will not fly until it is correctly balanced – it should hang horizontally when supported by the wingtips. Weight the nose until the proper balance is achieved by taping on strips of lead (you can find thin lead wrapped round the tops of some wine bottles). Or you can use large nails. Solder wire is ideal – but expensive.

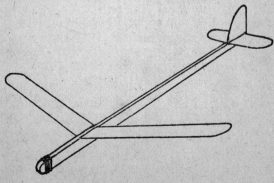

Football Rattle

YOU WILL NEED
Scraps of 6 mm plywood
Enamel paints
Strong string
Sandpaper

1 On a piece of 6 mm plywood, draw the shape shown. Cut it out, using a fretsaw.

SPECIAL EQUIPMENT
Clamps or a vice
A fretsaw
A drill

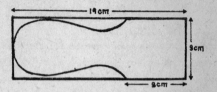

2 Cut out two squares of plywood, 8 cm × 8 cm. Sandpaper the edges and surfaces of the three pieces smooth.

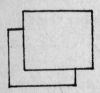

3 Clamp the pieces together firmly and drill two holes straight through all thicknesses 1 cm from the lower edge of the top piece, as shown. Paint the pieces in the colours of your favourite football team.

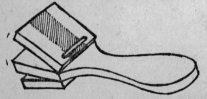

4 When the paint is dry, thread strong string through the holes and knot the ends so that the rattle is loosely held together.

Roll-A-Penny

YOU WILL NEED
A piece of hardboard 60 *cm*
  (24") *square*
A scrap of hardboard
180 *cm* (6') *of* 25 *mm* × 12 *mm*
  (1" × ½") *framework*
  battening
A piece of wood 20 *cm* × 6 *cm*
  × 2 *cm*
Wood glue
Sandpaper
Paints

SPECIAL EQUIPMENT
None

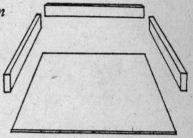

1 Cut the battening into
  three equal lengths and
  glue it along three sides of
  the smooth surface of the
  hardboard.

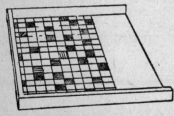

2 Paint the assembly with an
  undercoat and gloss paint.
  Leaving a 20 cm (8") wide
  strip along the open edge,
  divide the board into 4 cm
  squares and paint some of
  them different colours. Give
  each colour a number.

3 To make the channel of the
  penny roller, cut a triangle
  of hardboard to the
  measurements shown. Mark
  out the piece of wood as
  shown, and cut it in half.
  The two halves make the
  sides of the roller.

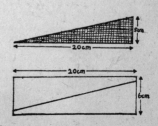

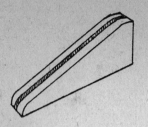

4 Glue the hardboard between the sides of the roller, and round off the lower ends with sandpaper.

5 Put the penny roller anywhere on the unsquared part of the board and try to land a 2p piece in one of the squares by rolling it down the channel.

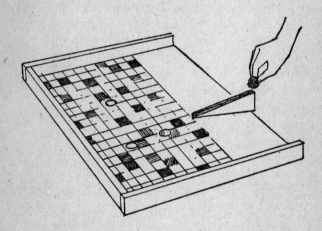

Double Bass

A tea chest made of plywood
A length of 25 mm (1″)
 square wood
Strong string
1½″ nails

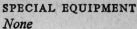

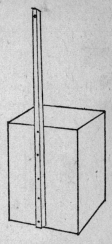

1 Drill a hole in one end of
the length of wood and nail
it to one side of the tea
chest.

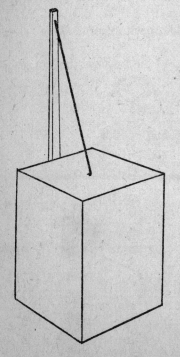

2 Drill a hole in the centre of
the top of the chest, tie a
knot in the string and
thread it through the hole
from the inside. Pass the
other end through the hole
in the wood, and tie it
tightly so that the string is
taut.

To play the double bass, put
one foot on the chest, and
bend the wood back while
twanging the string with
your other hand.

Blow Football

YOU WILL NEED
A large tray with raised edges
2 postcards
Sellotape
A ping pong ball
Drinking straws

SPECIAL EQUIPMENT
None

1 To make the goals, copy the shape shown on to two postcards and cut them out.

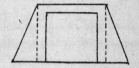

2 Score down the dotted lines with a sharp knife, held against a ruler, and bend the sides back to form wings.

3 Attach the goals to opposite ends of the tray with Sellotape.

The object of the game is for two (or more) players to blow the ping pong ball into their opponent's goal using a drinking straw.

Torpedo

YOU WILL NEED
*A metal cigar tube with a
   screw-on cap
Baking powder
Vinegar
A needle
Solder wire*

SPECIAL EQUIPMENT
None

1 Make a hole in the centre of the cap with a needle. Wrap a piece of solder wire round the middle of the cap.

2 Put equal quantities of baking powder and vinegar into the tube, replace the cap – QUICKLY – and launch your torpedo . . .

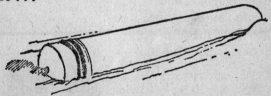

Spud Gun

YOU WILL NEED
A 22 cm (9") length of 6 mm brass tubing (obtainable from model shops)
A wooden ball
22 cm (9") of dowelling.or metal tubing, which must make a very good sliding fit inside the first tube
Wood glue

SPECIAL EQUIPMENT
A drill with a 5 mm bit

1 Drill a hole in the wooden ball and glue the dowelling firmly into it. (If you are using metal tubing instead of dowelling, block the other end of the tube with resin glue.)

2 Grease the dowelling and insert it into the brass tube. Stick the end of the tube into a potato, take aim — and fire!

36

Ring Board

YOU WILL NEED
A 50 cm (20") square of 1 cm
  thick plywood
8 right-angled hooks
6 rubber bottling rings
Gloss and enamel paints

SPECIAL EQUIPMENT
None

Give the board two coats of gloss paint. Then paint a face
and numbers on it as shown. Drill a small hole in the top
corner of the board. Screw a hook firmly above each number.
(If the tips of the screws go through to the back of the board,
hammer or file them flat.) Hang the board on a wall with a
piece of string through the hole, and see how many points you
can score by throwing the six rings over the hooks.

High Steppers

YOU WILL NEED
2 *empty tins with lids (e.g.*
   1 *litre paint tins)*
Strong string
Enamel paints

SPECIAL EQUIPMENT
None

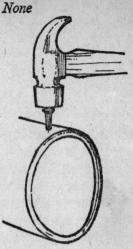

1 Pierce a hole with a nail in either side of each tin near the top. Don't do this without the lids in place or the tins may buckle.

2 Knot the end of two long pieces of string and thread them through one of the holes in each tin from the inside. Measure the length of string needed by standing on a tin and holding its string taut without bending over. Thread the string through the other hole from the outside and knot it to give the required length. Decorate the tins with enamel paints – and practise walking tall.

Picture Cube Game

YOU WILL NEED
12 *wooden child's playing
blocks or a 45 cm (18")
length of 35 mm (1½")
square "planed all round"
wood* *
6 *pictures cut from magazines,
approximately 12 cm ×
18 cm (5" × 7") in size*
Length of garter elastic
Wallpaper paste
Varnish

* *This size is slightly less than 35 mm
square*

SPECIAL EQUIPMENT
A trysquare
A sharp knife

1 If you don't have ready-made blocks, you will have to measure the exact width of your piece of wood, and mark off twelve lengths to that measurement. Saw the wood into twelve square pieces. Sandpaper all sides smooth.

See page 14 for how to saw cubes accurately.

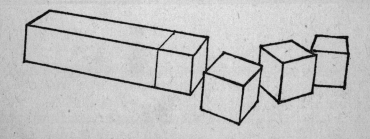

2 Make up some wallpaper paste. Dip the cubes into it and leave them to dry. (This will help the pictures to stick to the cubes later on.)

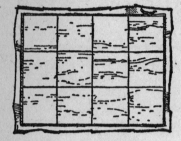

3 Put all your cubes together and bind them firmly round with the elastic. Paste the back of one of the magazine pictures, lay it flat on the table, face down, and place the block of cubes squarely on it.

4 Turn the cubes the other way up, and smooth out any wrinkles in the picture with your fingers. Make sure that the paper is stuck firmly to the wood all over. Leave the whole assembly to dry thoroughly.

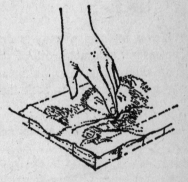

5 Putting the picture face down on the table again, trim the outside edges of it away from the cubes with a scalpel. Turn the block of cubes face up, and carefully slit the paper to separate the cubes. You may need to stick down some of the edges of the paper using a little paste on a paintbrush.

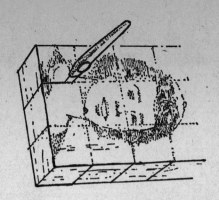

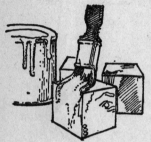

6 Repeat instructions 3 - 5 five times, pasting a different picture to each side of the block of cubes. When you have twelve paper-covered cubes, give each one a coat of varnish to protect the pictures.

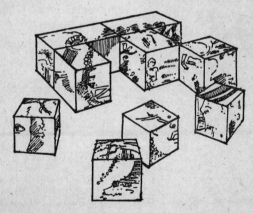

7 To play the picture cube game, tip all the cubes on to the table after shaking them up in a bag, and see how quickly you can fit a whole picture by re-throwing the cubes that don't match. Least number of throws wins.

Indoor House

YOU WILL NEED
A large table
Old sheets
Poster paints
Drawing pins or glue

SPECIAL EQUIPMENT
None

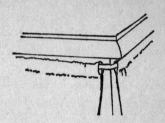

1 If it is an old table, pin the sheets all the way round it with drawing pins. Otherwise, use a latex glue, such as Copydex, to fix the sheets round the sides. (If you want to dismantle your house frequently, you could use a sewing machine to turn over a hem all the way along the top of the sheets, thread strong elastic through it, and tie the sheets round the table.)

2 Cut out window panes, or three sides of rectangles for window blinds and paint them. Cut a vertical slit in one sheet for the entrance. Paint your house with window boxes, creepers, drainpipes, a nameplate, etc.

Trick Bottle

YOU WILL NEED
A screw-top plastic bottle
A skewer or tapestry needle

SPECIAL EQUIPMENT
None

Ask someone to unscrew the top of this bottle for you, and they will suddenly find themselves sprayed with water!

1 Make several tiny holes in the bottom and round the base of the bottle with the skewer.

2 Fill the bottle with water right up to the top and quickly screw on the cap. No water will escape through the holes until the cap is removed.

Ventriloquist's Snake

YOU WILL NEED

An old pair of thick, brightly-coloured tights
An egg box
Scraps of foam rubber
Scraps of felt
Embroidery silk
Copydex
The ability to talk without moving your lips!

SPECIAL EQUIPMENT
None

1 Cut one leg and half the other leg's foot from the tights.

2 Make a cut across the heel of the leg and sew the toe piece into the hole, as shown. This makes the snake's upper and lower jaws.

3 Cut two pieces of foam rubber to fit inside the upper jaw and two pieces to fit inside the lower jaw. Your fingers and thumb should fit neatly into the space left inside the head.

4 Cut half of two cups from the egg box for the snake's eyes and fit them between the foam rubber and the material of the upper jaw. Glue all the foam and the eyes in place with Copydex.

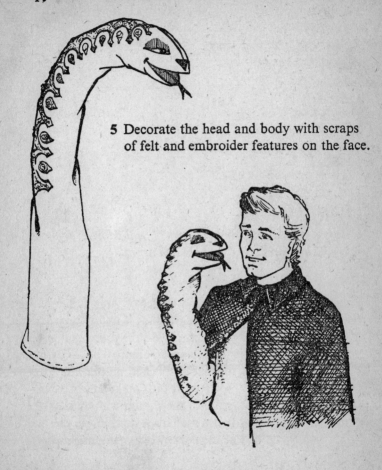

5 Decorate the head and body with scraps of felt and embroider features on the face.

6 Put your hand inside the head and pull the body all the way up your arm. Wear a cape to hide the end of the snake's body – and start practising your act.

Magic Coin Trick

YOU WILL NEED
A postcard
A piece of 1 mm thick card
   10 cm × 18 mm
A very small cloth bag
Hat elastic
A matchbox
A slightly larger box
Rubber bands
Sellotape

SPECIAL EQUIPMENT
None

*This is a simple conjuring trick which will baffle everyone –
and which you can repeat again and again.*

How the trick appears: Ask a member of your audience for a
halfpenny, and tell him or her to mark it in any way he likes
so that he can identify it later. Hold it in your hand and say
you are going to tie it up in a special money bag – by magic.
Put the halfpenny in your jacket pocket, mutter a few magic
spells, and then, with a "Hey presto!", take out of your
pocket a small box. Give it to the person who marked the
coin. Inside it he will find a matchbox, and inside the matchbox a small bag, tied at the neck, which contains his halfpenny.
How it's done: To "magic" the coin into the bag, you push it
down a cardboard slide, hidden in your pocket, which is
inserted into the neck of the bag, through the mouth of the
matchbox and the outer box. (It's a good idea to practise the
trick several times before trying it out on an audience.)

1 Using the piece of thick card, cut to the same width as a halfpenny, as a "former", fold the postcard tightly round it, and wrap it with several layers of Sellotape. Take out the "former". A halfpenny should slide easily through the flat postcard tube.

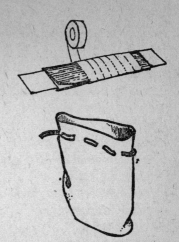

2 If you cannot find a suitable small bag, make one out of cloth. Thread a large-eyed needle with hat elastic, and tack round the neck of the bag. Insert the cardboard tube and pull the elastic tight round it. Tie the ends in a knot.

3 Put the bag inside the matchbox with the slide protruding, and wrap several rubber bands round the outside. Put the matchbox inside the larger box. Put it in your pocket.

4 When you put the marked halfpenny in your pocket, secretly drop it down the slide into the bag, and pull out the slide, leaving it in your pocket. The bag will close up, and the rubber bands will snap the matchbox shut. Close the outer box at the same time, and when you hand it to your audience, there will be no sign of how the coin found its way into the bag.

Feeding Time

YOU WILL NEED

*A piece of wood or hardboard,
    approximately 90 cm ×
    30 cm (36" × 12")*
*A length of catapult elastic
    (available from model shops)*
2 15 cm (6") nails
*Cardboard tubes from inside
    rolls of kitchen paper.*
Toilet roll tubes
Poster paints

SPECIAL EQUIPMENT
None

1 Cut a circular hole in one
side of each tube. Paint the
tubes to look like animal
faces, using the holes as
mouths.

2 Hammer the nails into one
end of the piece of wood,
12 cm (5") apart, and attach
the elastic as shown.

3 Tape or glue your animals
firmly to the other end of
the wooden base, and "feed"
them with paper pellets fired
from the elastic catapult.
Score different points for
feeding each animal.

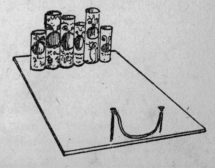

Woolly Owl

YOU WILL NEED
1 oz dark brown wool
1 oz light brown wool
Cardboard
Scraps of felt or 2 small,
   round black buttons
String

SPECIAL EQUIPMENT
Tapestry needle

1 Cut two discs of cardboard measuring approximately 9 cm across with a centre hole of 4.5 cm across.

2 Put the two discs together and wind the wool round and round them, using both colours at the same time. Continue winding the wool until the centre hole is completely filled. You will need a large needle to finish it off.

3 Using scissors or a sharp knife, cut the wool around the edge of the cardboard discs.

4 Tie a piece of light string tightly between the two discs. Cut the discs away and fluff out the woolly ball so that it has a flat base.

5 Sew on two small buttons or scraps of felt for eyes, and sew or glue on scraps of felt for your owl's beak and feet.

Ping Pong Bats and Net

YOU WILL NEED
4 *mm plywood*
A piece of 6 *mm wood* 48 *cm*
  × 25 *mm*
Medium grade sandpaper
Wood glue
2 *G clamps*
2 *shelf brackets*
A piece of old sheet
Coloured plastic tape
String
Varnish

SPECIAL EQUIPMENT
A fretsaw
A chisel
A sewing machine

1 Using a fretsaw, cut out
  two 20 cm circles of plywood
  and sandpaper the edges
  smooth. Glue a 20 cm circle
  of medium grade sandpaper
  to each side.

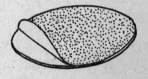

2 To make handles for the
  bats, cut the wood into four
  12 cm lengths. Using a
  chisel, round off each piece
  at the sides and at one end
  to make the shapes shown.
  Sandpaper each piece
  smooth.

3 Cut out two pieces of plywood, 10 cm × 25 mm. Glue each piece between two of the half-handles, as shown, using clamps to grip each assembly together until they are firmly cemented.

4 Now glue the faces of the bats into the handles, again using clamps while the glue is drying. Decorate the handles by wrapping coloured tape round them.

5 For the net, cut a length of thin cloth (an old sheet would be ideal) approximately 1.2 metres × 20 cm (4′ × 8″). Hem the two short edges. Turn over 25 mm (1″) hems on the long sides and stitch them 12 mm (½″) from the edge, Thread a long piece of string through each hem, leaving at least 30 cm (12″) to spare at both ends.

6 Drill a hole in each shelf
bracket near the corner
and in the middle of one
arm, 15 cm from the first.

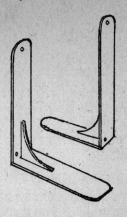

7 Fix the brackets to either side of a rectangular table with
the G clamps, and thread the net strings through the
holes, tying them together so that the net is stretched taut.

Monkey Seat

YOU WILL NEED
Square of 18 mm (¾") plywood
   35 cm × 35 cm (14" × 14")
Length of thick nylon rope
Nail and string
Polyurethane varnish
Sandpaper

SPECIAL EQUIPMENT
A padsaw
A drill with a 15 mm bit

1 Knock a nail halfway into the centre of the plywood. Make a loop in one end of a piece of string, put the loop over the nail, and tie the string to a pencil exactly 16 cm (6½") away from the nail. Mark out a circle on the wood, as shown.

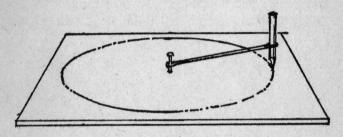

2 Cut out the circle you have marked, using a padsaw. Drill a hole 15 mm in diameter in the centre of the circle. Sandpaper the edges and all surfaces of the wood very thoroughly, so that the seat is perfectly smooth. Paint it with at least two coats of varnish.

3 Knot the rope with a very large, tight knot about 30 cm (12″) from one end. Thread the other end through the seat. Singe both ends of the rope to stop it fraying.

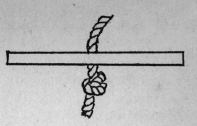

4 Get an adult to help you hang your seat from a strong tree branch in a place where it can swing safely without encountering any obstacles.

Snake-in-the-Box

YOU WILL NEED
Scraps of plywood
Material
Wood glue
Panel pins
A screw eye and hook
Foam rubber scraps
Paints or coloured paper

SPECIAL EQUIPMENT
A sewing machine would be useful

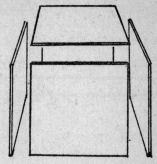

1 Make a 15 cm square box, using panel pins and glue, out of five pieces of wood.

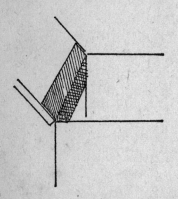

2 Cut a strip of cloth and glue it along the lid and one side of the box to form a hinge.

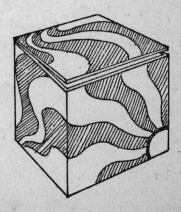

3 Paint the box – or cover it with wallpaper, Fablon, or cut-out pictures – inside and out.

4 Make a tube out of a long piece of material by sewing the edges together and turning it inside out.

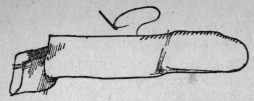

5 Stuff the tube with foam scraps, sew up the end, and embroider eyes and a mouth to make it look like a silly snake.

6 Pack it into the box, close the lid – and give it to an unsuspecting friend to open . . .

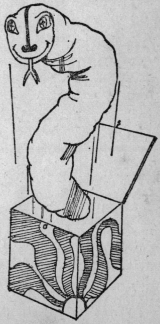

Bar Skittles

YOU WILL NEED
A broomstick
A square of 12 mm chipboard
9 drawing pins
9 small, cylindrical cartons
A small, solid rubber ball
Strong adhesive
String
A nail
A paper clip
A wood screw

SPECIAL EQUIPMENT
None

1 Screw the broomstick to one corner of the board.

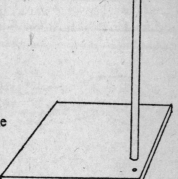

2 Stick the drawing pins into the board in the pattern shown.

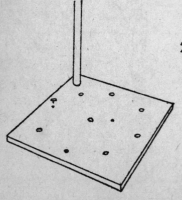

3 Make a hole in the ball with a gimlet or a small screw-driver. Coat one end of a length of string with strong adhesive and push it into the ball with a matchstick. Make sure it is very firmly fixed. Knock a nail halfway into the top of the broomstick. Tie the other end of the string to a paper clip, and drop the clip over the nail. The length of the string must be just the amount necessary to let the ball touch the furthest carton when they are set out on the board.

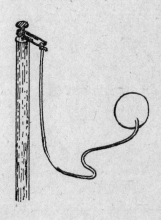

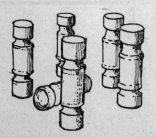

4 Spice containers make ideal skittles. Remove the lids and cover each one with coloured paper. Place them upside down on the drawing pin markers.

5 The object of the game is to knock all the skittles down with as few swings of the ball as possible.

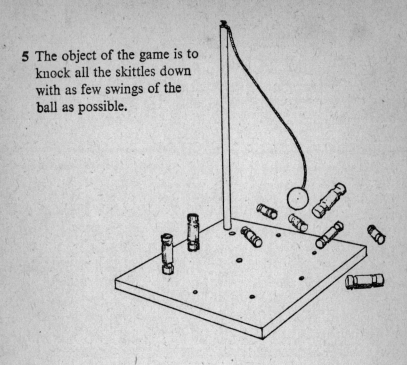

Name Stamp

YOU WILL NEED
Scrap of soft lino
Ink pad
Scrap of wood
Cupboard door knob
Glue

SPECIAL EQUIPMENT
A lino-cutting tool
A sharp knife

1 Using a sharp knife and a ruler, cut a rectangle of lino to fit the surface of the ink pad.

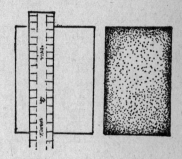

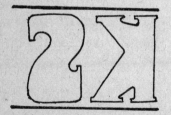

2 Draw the initials of your name, or your christian name if it's not too long, *backwards* on to the surface of the lino.

3 With a lino-cutting tool, neatly cut out the lino round the letters, leaving them standing up in relief. (Don't dig the tool too deeply into the surface or it will probably slip.)

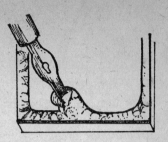

4 Cut a block of wood, about 15 mm thick, to the size of the piece of lino. Sandpaper the edges and glue it to the back of the lino. You can paint it a bright colour, if you like.

5 Screw the cupboard door knob into the middle of the wood block.

Why not make a set of different stamps for all sorts of occasions?

Cartesian Diver

YOU WILL NEED

*A tall glass jar (a spaghetti jar,
  if you have one, is ideal)*
A balloon
A very small bottle
Sellotape

SPECIAL EQUIPMENT

None

1 Make a diver out of a
small bottle which, when
partly filled, barely floats on
the surface of water.

2 Fill the jar with water to
about an inch below the
rim. Float your diver on the
surface, and stretch a
balloon over the top of the
jar, sealing it round the
outside with Sellotape.
When you press down on
the balloon with your
fingers, the diver will
slowly sink.

Zither

YOU WILL NEED

2 *pieces of thin plywood, 32 cm*
   × 8 cm
80 *cm of 6 mm square wood*
A 32 cm length of 6 mm ×
   4 mm wood
Sandpaper
Wood glue
Panel pins
16 *screw eyes*
4.5 *metres* (15′) *of piano or*
   guitar wire
Enamel paints

SPECIAL EQUIPMENT

A fretsaw or padsaw

1 Draw a circle with a radius
of 25 mm (1″) in the centre
of one piece of plywood,
and cut it out carefully
with the fretsaw. Sandpaper
the edge smooth.

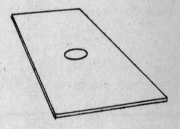

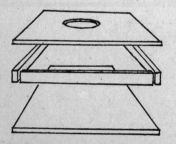

2 Cut the length of wood into
four pieces, and, using panel
pins and glue, join them to
the two pieces of ply, as
shown.

3 Glue the 6 mm × 4 mm piece of wood across the top of the zither, 25 mm (1″) from one edge.

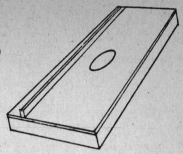

4 Starting 5 mm from either end, mark out sixteen points, 2 cm apart, down the long sides of the top of the zither. On the points opposite the "bridge", knock in 16 panel pins at a slight angle, as shown. Screw in a screw eye on each point marked behind the "bridge"

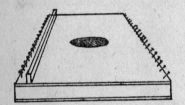

The zither can be painted before you string it.

5 Cut the wire into sixteen equal lengths and make a small, neat loop at one end of each piece. Hook each loop over a panel pin and attach the other end to the opposite screw eye.

The zither can be played with your fingers or with a guitar plectrum. Adjust the notes by tightening and loosening the screw eyes.

Money Bucket

YOU WILL NEED
A large metal bucket
Gloss paints
Coins

SPECIAL EQUIPMENT
None

1 Paint the bottom of the bucket in bright colours with the pattern shown.

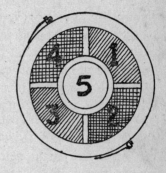

2 When the paint is dry completely fill the bucket with water. The object of the game is to drop coins into the bucket so that they land on the numbered sections – and do not touch any of the lines.

Hula Hoop Goal-scoring

YOU WILL NEED
A hula hoop
2 posts
String
A football
Bricks

SPECIAL EQUIPMENT
None

Fix the posts firmly into the ground the correct distance
apart. (Lay them on the ground with the hoop between
them first to measure the distance.) Tie the hoop
to the posts with four pieces of string.
Make a line on the ground 15 metres away from the goal.
Place the bricks on the ground 10 metres in front of the
line, and take it in turns to score from there. Whenever
you score, move your brick one metre further back. The
first player to score from the back line is the winner.

Automatic Dice-shaker

YOU WILL NEED
Small, clear plastic box with
 lid (the sort used for
 packaging fragile objects, e.g.
 flowers, powder puffs, etc)
Scrap of felt
2 large dice
Glue

SPECIAL EQUIPMENT
None

1 Put the dice into the box and neatly tape the lid on with Sellotape.

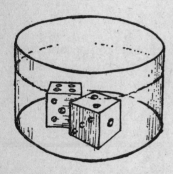

2 Cut a piece of felt to fit the base of the box, stick it on with glue – and your dice-shaker is ready for action.

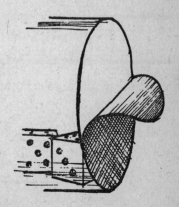

Felt Doll and Dress

YOU WILL NEED
For the doll:
45 cm (18″) square of flesh-
    coloured felt
Matching thread
Stuffing
Thick wool for hair
Scrap of ribbon
Embroidery silk or felt scraps
    for features

For the dress:
Piece of fabric 30 cm ×
    50 cm (12″ × 20″)
Frilled lace (optional)
Hook and eye fastener

SPECIAL EQUIPMENT
*A sewing machine would be
    useful*

1 Draw the three patterns shown opposite to the correct size
  on to pieces of paper and cut them out. Pin the patterns
  to the felt and cut out two bodies, four arms and four legs.

2 Pin the arm pieces together in pairs and oversew all
  round, leaving the ends open. Do the same with the leg
  pieces. Pin the two body pieces together and oversew all
  round, leaving the bottom open.

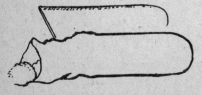

3 Stuff the arms and legs and
  sew up the ends.

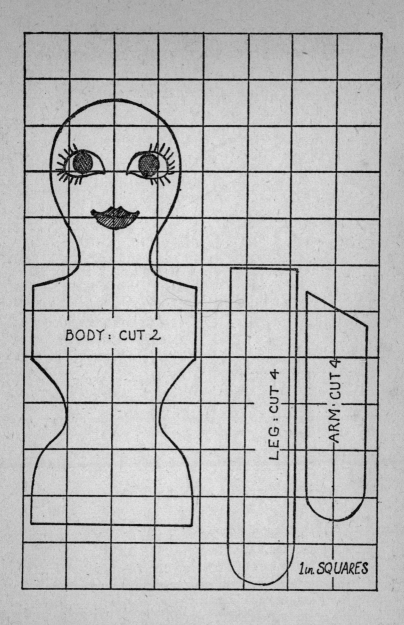

BODY : CUT 2

LEG : CUT 4

ARM : CUT 4

1in. SQUARES

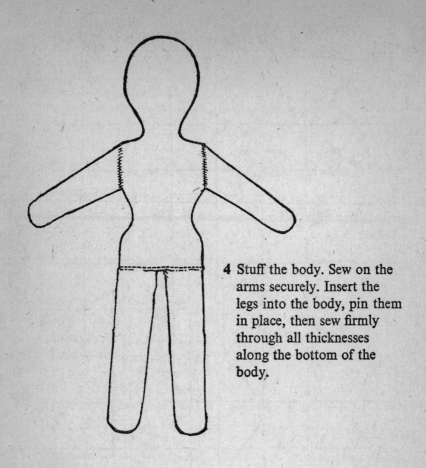

4 Stuff the body. Sew on the arms securely. Insert the legs into the body, pin them in place, then sew firmly through all thicknesses along the bottom of the body.

5 For the hair, cut lots of 30 cm (12″) lengths of wool. Divide them into several bunches and tie each bunch in the centre with another 30 cm length.

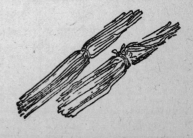

6 Thread a large needle with the same wool. Pin the bunches of hair to the head and sew each one on with wool, through the centre knots. Sew some strands of hair to the back of the head. Tie the hair in bunches with ribbon. Sew eyes, a nose and a mouth on to the doll's face with embroidery silk, or cut out scraps of felt for features and sew them in place.

7 *For the dress:* trace the bodice patterns shown on to pieces of paper. Pin them on to your fabric and cut out one front and two back bodice pieces. Cut a straight piece of fabric 20 cm × 50 cm (8″ × 20″) for the skirt.

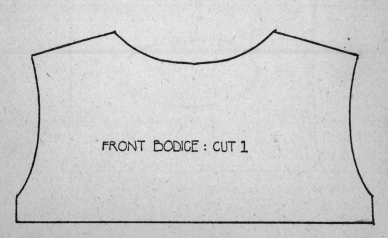

FRONT BODICE : CUT 1

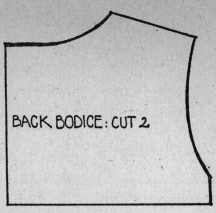

BACK BODICE: CUT 2

8 Fold over 5 mm ($\frac{1}{4}''$) on the straight edge of each back
bodice piece and sew. Put the back and front bodice
pieces right sides together and sew the shoulder seams.
Turn over 5 mm ($\frac{1}{4}''$) round the neck and armholes and sew.
You can sew on pre-frilled lace round the neck and arms
if you like. Sew the side seams on the bodice.

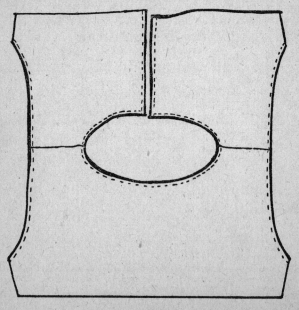

9 Sew the 20 cm edges of the large piece of fabric together. Turn up a 1 cm hem and sew it neatly. Tack along the top edge of the skirt and gather it up.

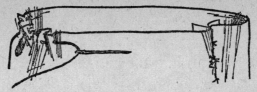

10 Fit the bottom edge of the bodice to the gathered edge, right sides together. Pin and sew. Sew a hook and eye fastener to the top of the back opening.

11 You can complete your doll by adding extra details if you
like.

Ostrich Puppet

YOU WILL NEED
A tennis ball
A ping pong ball
Thin rope
2 screw-on bottle caps
Feathers or felt scraps
Scraps of wood
5 screw eyes
Cotton
Pins

SPECIAL EQUIPMENT
None

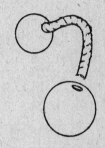

1 Make a small hole in each of the balls and glue either end of a short piece of rope (washing-line thickness is best) into the holes.

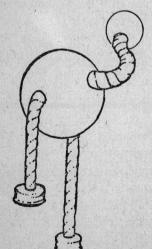

2 Cut two lengths of rope for legs and glue on the bottle caps for feet. Make two more holes in the tennis ball and glue in the legs.

3 Glue on feathers (or cut-out felt shapes) for wings and tail, and a paper beak and eyes.

4 Nail three pieces of wood together to form a crosspiece, as shown, and screw in the screw eyes at the points marked.

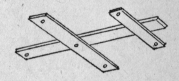

5 Stick pins into the ostrich's body at the neck and tail. Tie cotton to the pins and to each knee. Thread a long needle and pass it through the head. Tie the end of each piece of cotton to its corresponding screw eye on the crosspiece.

Draughts or Chess Board

YOU WILL NEED
Smooth floor tile 30 cm (12")
  square.
40 cm × 40 cm (18" × 18")
  white Fablon
40 cm × 12 cm (18" × 5")
  black Fablon
40 cm × 40 cm (18" × 18")
  clear Fablon
30 cm × 30 cm (12" × 12")
  stick-on baize

SPECIAL EQUIPMENT
None

1 Cover the floor tile with the white Fablon, cutting off the corners and sticking the spare edges to the back.

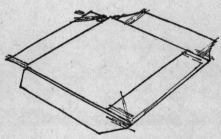

2 Lightly rule the surface of the board into 1½" squares.

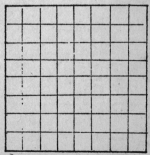

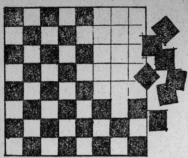

3 Rule the back of the piece of black Fablon into 32 1½″ squares. Cut them out accurately. Peel off the backing paper and stick them in a chequered pattern on the squares ruled on the board.

4 Cover the chequered board with the clear Fablon. Roll it on and smooth it out carefully so as not to leave air pockets. Cut off the corners and stick the spare edges to the back of the board.

5 Finish by sticking a square of baize Fablon to the bottom of your board.

Draughtsmen

YOU WILL NEED
DAS modelling material
Rolling pin
Small scone-cutter or napkin
  ring
Poster paints
Varnish
Small box

SPECIAL EQUIPMENT
None

1 Roll out the DAS with the rolling pin to an even thickness of 3 mm. With the scone-cutter, neatly cut out twenty-four circles. Leave the circles to dry thoroughly.

2 When dry, paint twelve of the draughts black, and twelve of them white, with poster paints. (Or you can paint them in bright colours if you wish.)

3 When the paint has dried, give each one a coat of varnish.

4 Find a small box to keep your draughts in. If you like, you can cover it with paper and decorate it in a chequered pattern.

Catch the Rat

YOU WILL NEED
A long plank
A length of plastic drainpipe
A stepladder
A block of wood
A stick
Wire or string

SPECIAL EQUIPMENT
None

This is a silly game to test your quick reflexes!

Tie the drainpipe firmly to the plank, and fix the plank to the top of the stepladder. Drop the "rat" into the pipe – the "ratcatcher" must hit it with the stick as it shoots out of the bottom end.

Swanee Whistle

YOU WILL NEED
25 cm (10") of 25 mm (1")
   diameter plastic plumbing
   pipe
6 cm (2½") of dowelling*
Scrap of felt
A metal washer
Length of straight, thick
   wire
A small screw
Glue

SPECIAL EQUIPMENT
A drill
A file

The dowelling must be exactly the right size to fit snugly inside the pipe, but able to slide smoothly up and down. You may have to sandpaper it slightly, all over, to achieve this.

1 Saw off one end of the pipe at an angle, as shown. 15 mm from this end, make a careful cut halfway through the tube at right angles. Then cut down towards the first cut, at a slant, as shown.

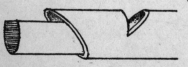

2 Cut a 15 mm length of dowelling and file it flat by about 2 mm. Push it into the mouthpiece of the pipe and glue it in place. One end of the dowelling should be in line with the vertical cut in the pipe.

3 Cut off the other end of the
dowelling at the same angle
as the pipe, and then cut
the pipe and dowelling
vertically, 5 mm from the
end.

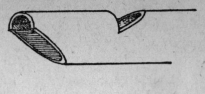

4 To make a bung for the whistle, cut a 25 mm length of
dowelling and drill a hole in one end the same size as the
thickness of the wire. Cut a circle of felt (leather or rubber
will also do) fractionally larger than the diameter of the
dowelling. Your washer must be fractionally smaller. Screw
washer and felt to the other end of the dowelling. Glue
the wire into the hole.

5 Drill a hole through the remaining piece of dowelling large
enough for the wire to slide through freely. Slide it up the
wire, and plug it into the end of the whistle, glueing it firmly
in place. Bend the end of the wire with pliers to form a loop
for your fingers.

By blowing through the mouthpiece and sliding the bung up
and down, you should be able to play two octaves on your
whistle.

Solitaire

YOU WILL NEED
2 *pieces of 6 mm plywood,*
  22 cm square
48 *cm of 6 mm dowelling*
Sandpaper
Wood glue

SPECIAL EQUIPMENT
A drill with a 6 mm bit

1 Sandpaper the edges of both boards smooth. With a ruler, carefully mark off one board into 1.5 cm squares.

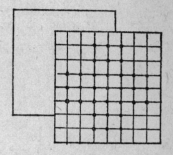

2 Drill 33 holes right through the board, at the points shown.

3 Glue the boards together, and sandpaper the edges and the top.

4 To make the pegs, cut the dowelling into 32 15 mm lengths. You may need to sandpaper the ends to make them all fit neatly into the holes.

5 To play solitaire, plug in all the pegs, leaving the centre hole empty. The object of the game is to eliminate the pegs from the board by jumping them, in turn, over one another (vertically or horizontally, but not diagonally), until you have only one peg left, in the centre hole.

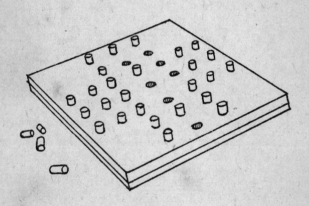

Secret Book Safe

YOU WILL NEED

A large, very thick, hardback book, in reasonably good condition. Buy one cheaply at a second-hand bookshop or jumble sale

Scraps of felt

Copydex

SPECIAL EQUIPMENT

A sharp knife

3 clamps

1 Open the book at page 40 or so. Mark a rectangle on the right-hand page a ruler's width from the edges. With a sharp knife, cut along the ruled lines to a depth of about 25 mm (1"). (You may only be able to cut through half the required thickness of pages at a time.)

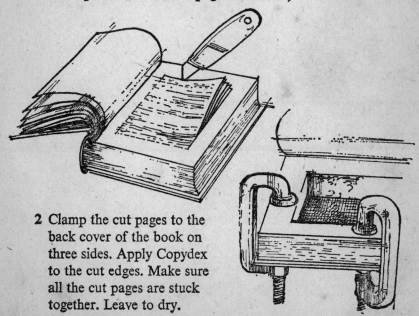

2 Clamp the cut pages to the back cover of the book on three sides. Apply Copydex to the cut edges. Make sure all the cut pages are stuck together. Leave to dry.

3 Cut out five pieces of felt (or velvet) to fit the bottom and sides of the hole you have cut out. Using Copydex, stick them in place. When the glue is dry, remove the clamps.

4 Now hide your jewels in the book safe, and put it on the bookshelf.

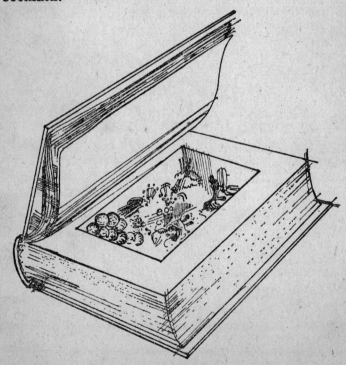

Dracula Mask

YOU WILL NEED
Plenty of Plasticine or clay
Vaseline
Newspaper
Flour and water
Poster paints
Hat elastic

SPECIAL EQUIPMENT
None

1 First, measure the dimensions of your face – from ear to ear, and top of head to chin. On a board, build a lump of Plasticine into a model of Dracula's face to the same size as your own. Cover it with a coat of Vaseline.

2 Tear newspaper into small pieces and paste them all over the model with flour-and-water paste. Give it plenty of layers. Leave to dry thoroughly.

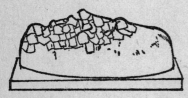

3 Scrape all the Plasticine from inside the mask, and, if necessary, give the outside a final, smooth layer of paper and paste.

4 Paint Dracula's face dead white, with blood-red lips and
gleaming fangs. Give him black-as-night hair, and bloodshot
eyes. Pierce a hole on either side of the mask, thread a length
of hat elastic through the holes and knot the ends on the
inside.

Comedy Show

YOU WILL NEED
An assistant
A table, with curtains behind it
Baby clothes
Stuffing or newspaper
Safety pins
A pair of shoes, gloves and a
  hat or wig

SPECIAL EQUIPMENT
None

Pin the curtains together, leaving gaps for your head, hands, and your assistant's hands to stick through. Stuff the baby clothes and pin them to the front of the curtains, and put a pair of shoes on the table. Stick your head – wearing a hat or a wig – through the top gap, and your gloved hands through the next. Your assistant operates the shoes through the lower gap. Put on a funny voice, and make the "baby" do a comedy act.

Crazy Golf Course

YOU WILL NEED
Planks, drainpipes, bricks, boxes, flowerpots, etc.

SPECIAL EQUIPMENT
None

If you have a golf club, a golf ball, and a garden, you can have great fun designing your own crazy golf course. (This game can also be played with croquet or tennis racquets, or even round the house.) Here are some suggestions for crazy obstacles:

1 A piece of drainpipe laid along the ground, held in place by bricks.

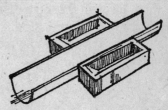

2 A croquet hoop with a swinging board hanging 1″ from the ground.

3 A cardboard box with mouseholes cut into the sides.

4 A see-saw made of a thin plank, or a piece of strong cardboard, balanced on a round log (a large jam jar will do).

5 A bridge, made from two plank ramps and a length of drainpipe balanced on bricks.

6 A walk-the-plank obstacle, fixed over a step with a flowerpot placed underneath it.

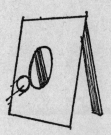

7 An old sheet, or a large piece of hardboard, with a hole cut in it.

Lawn Darts

YOU WILL NEED
3 *hollow rubber balls*
Polyfilla
Dowelling
A piece of thick plastic sheet

SPECIAL EQUIPMENT
None

1 Cut the dowelling into three equal lengths of approximately 18 cm (7"). At one end of each, make two crosswise cuts about 10 cm (4") deep.

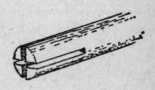

2 Cut a small circular hole in each ball, of the same diameter as the dowelling. Mix a quantity of Polyfilla, pack an equal amount into each ball, and embed a piece of dowelling in it through the hole. The dowelling shafts should stick out about 10 cm (4"). Put the darts in an airing cupboard or on top of a boiler to make the Polyfilla dry more quickly.

3 Cut two 15 cm squares of
plastic sheet (the sort
fertilizer bags are made of).
Fold each one in half
horizontally, vertically and
diagonally.

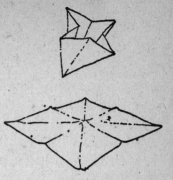

4 Hold each square by the centre and push the middles of
the outside edges together. They will fold into four-winged
dart shapes. Glue the inside surfaces of each dart together
and glue one into the slots cut in each dowelling shaft.
Mark out circular targets on the lawn – and aim the darts
at them from at least five yards away.

Magic Money-Maker

YOU WILL NEED
2 10 cm (4") lengths of broom
   handle (25 mm (1")
   dowelling)
Scraps of wood
Length of paper about 10 cm
   (4") wide
Coat hanger
Screws and nails
Sandpaper
Glue
Paint
Any banknote

SPECIAL EQUIPMENT
A drill

This little toy apparently turns blank paper into real money!

1 To make the base and
   sides for your Money-
   Maker, first cut out two pieces
   of wood approximately
   10 cm × 5 cm (4" × 2").
   Rule a line down the
   centre of each one and mark
   two points on the line 35 mm
   apart, equi-distant from
   each end, as shown. Drill
   small holes through the
   wood at each of these
   points.

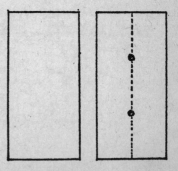

2 Cut a piece of wood to a suitable size for your base, and screw the side pieces on to it, 10.5 cm apart (just over the length of the pieces of broom handle). Sandpaper all the edges smooth. Paint the assembly with two coats of gloss paint.

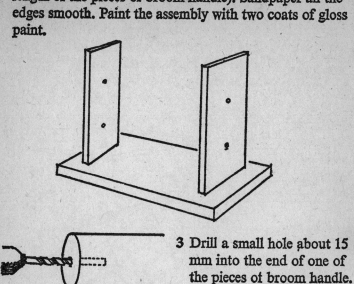

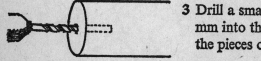

3 Drill a small hole about 15 mm into the end of one of the pieces of broom handle.

4 Glue one end of a long piece of paper along one of the pieces of broom handle. It must be glued perfectly straight so that the paper can be rolled straight round the wood. Glue the other end of the paper along the second broom handle – *so that it rolls in the opposite direction to the first,* as shown.

5 Fit the two rollers between the sides of the base assembly, with the drilled one on top. Fix them in place with nails knocked into the centre of each roller through the holes in the sides – except where you have drilled a hole. Here, glue a piece of coat hanger wire into the hole in the roller, through the hole in the side piece, and shape it into a handle with a pair of pliers. The whole assembly should be loose, so that the rollers rotate freely.

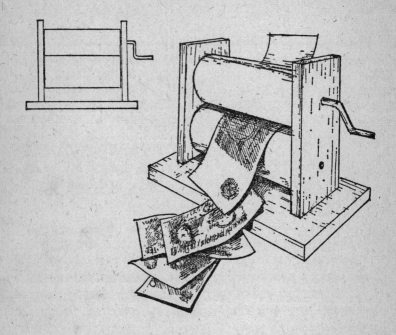

6 To operate your Magic Money-Maker, wind the paper on to one of the rollers as far as you can, insert a banknote, and wind the rollers back until the note is hidden inside the rolled paper. Now take a piece of blank paper of roughly the size of the note, insert it into the other side of the Money-Maker, wind it into the assembly, and – hey presto! – a real banknote will come out the other side.

Pair of Maracas

YOU WILL NEED
2 *balloons*
Vaseline
Newspaper
Flour and water
Some coffee beans
Enamel paints
A 40 cm (16") length of dowelling

SPECIAL EQUIPMENT
None

1 Blow up the balloons until they are both about the size of a small melon. Tie a knot in the neck of each and cover them all over with a coat of Vaseline.

2 Mix the flour and water into a thickish paste. Tear the newspaper into short strips and paste these all over the balloons. Give each balloon at least five layers of paper. Leave them to dry out completely.

3 Stick a small piece of Sellotape over the uncovered part of each balloon's neck. Pierce the balloons with a pin through the Sellotape. This will let the air escape slowly. Remove the balloons from their paper shells. Put a handful of coffee beans into each shell.

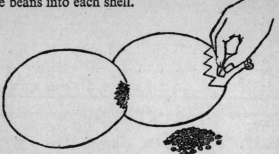

4 Saw the length of dowelling in half, and paste the neck of the shells to the dowelling with more strips of newspaper. Use plenty of layers. Leave the maracas to dry thoroughly.

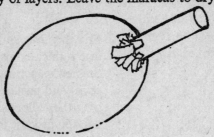

5 Paint your maracas with undercoat or emulsion, then decorate with bright enamel paints.

Crazy Car Race

YOU WILL NEED
A length of wood, about 60 cm
  × 10 cm (24″ × 4″)
Plywood
Battening
Sandpaper
Wood glue
2 G clamps
Dinky toys
A large board

SPECIAL EQUIPMENT
A coping saw

1 Draw four or five tunnel outlines on to the wood and cut them out with the coping saw. Sandpaper the edges.

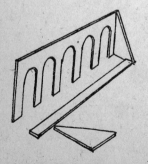

2 Cut two triangular wings for the tunnel board out of plywood, and glue one to each end. Attach a length of battening to the bottom of the wings to stop the cars when they go through the tunnels.

101

3 Fix the board to one end of a table with the G clamps. Raise the other end of the board and race toy cars down it, aiming for the tunnels.

Soap Racing Yacht

YOU WILL NEED
Scrap of balsa wood
A cocktail stick
A piece of paper
A sliver of soap

SPECIAL EQUIPMENT
None

1 Cut a boat shape about 5 cm (2″) long out of the balsa, and make a narrow notch at the back end.

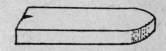

2 Cut out a square of paper for the sail and attach it to the boat with a cocktail stick.

3 Stick a piece of soap into the notch – and set sail. The melting soap will cause the boat to move across the water.

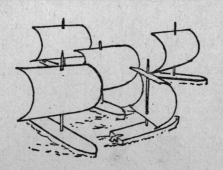

Doll's Fourposter

YOU WILL NEED
A shoe box with lid
A piece of card
Approx. 1 metre (3') of
    dowelling
Glue
Scraps of fabric
Sewing materials

SPECIAL EQUIPMENT
None

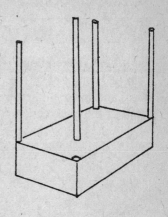

1 Turn the box upside down, and make a hole in each corner. Cut the dowelling into four equal lengths and glue a piece through each hole to the inside of the box.

2 Cut out a piece of card to the right size and glue it to one end of the assembly.

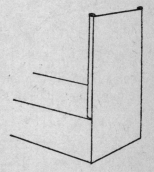

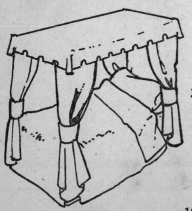

3 Glue the box lid to the top of the posts. Glue material over the lid and make curtains to tie round the posts. Make bedclothes out of scraps of material.

Doll's Carrycot

YOU WILL NEED
A strong shoe box
A large piece of Fablon
About 1½ metres of tape
Coloured Sellotape or braid
Scraps of material

SPECIAL EQUIPMENT
None

1 Measure your shoe box, and work out how much Fablon you will need to cover the bottom, sides, and most of the inside. Cut your piece of Fablon to the required shape, as shown.

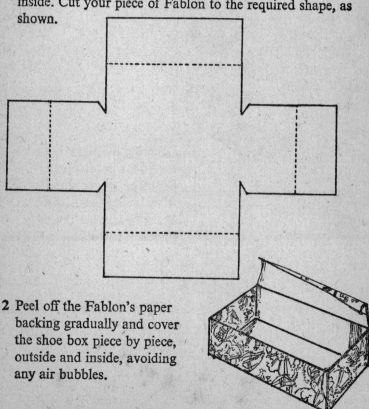

2 Peel off the Fablon's paper backing gradually and cover the shoe box piece by piece, outside and inside, avoiding any air bubbles.

3 Take a length of tape and fix it over the bottom of the box, with pieces of left-over Fablon, to make the carrying handles.

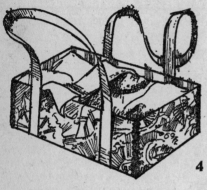

4 Decorate the edges of the carrycot with coloured Sellotape, or stick on braid with double-sided Sellotape. Make bedclothes out of scraps of material.

Womble Mask

YOU WILL NEED
Strong card
Felt
Sellotape
Braid
Copydex
Wool
Wire
Black plastic insulating tape
Hat elastic

SPECIAL EQUIPMENT
None

1 To make Uncle Bulgaria's hat, cut out a disc of card to fit the top of your head, and cut a strip of card 5 cm (2″) wide, long enough to encircle the disc. Cut out a disc and strip of coloured felt to the same size. Attach the strip of card to the card disc with Sellotape inside and out.

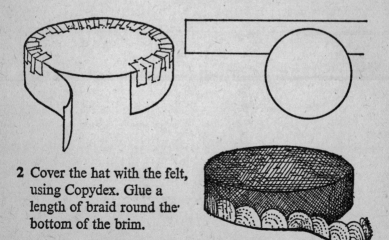

2 Cover the hat with the felt, using Copydex. Glue a length of braid round the bottom of the brim.

3 Make a tassel Attach the tassel to the centre of the hat with a length of plaited wool.

4 Cut out a long triangular piece of card with a base long enough to fit halfway round the hat brim. Cover it with yellow felt, using Copydex. Stick a little triangle of black felt at the tip for a nose.

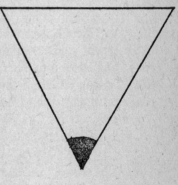

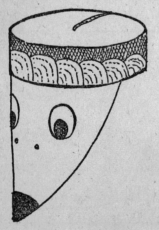

5 Glue the yellow triangle inside the hat brim. Make eyes out of scraps of felt and stick them in place. Pierce tiny holes in the nose through which to see.

6 Make spectacles out of wire, twisted into shape with pliers, and bind them with black plastic tape. Stitch them on to the mask. Glue wool hair round the back and sides of the hat brim. To keep the mask in place, attach a piece of hat elastic inside the hat to go under your chin.

Open-ended Tent

YOU WILL NEED
A large piece of heavy-duty
  polythene sheet
4 lengths of thick string or
  rope
10 15 cm (6″) nails
2 stout poles

SPECIAL EQUIPMENT
None

Drive the poles firmly into the ground so that they stand
upright. The distance between them should be the width of
the sheet. Nail the sheet to the top of the uprights. Tie two
guy ropes to each nail and nail them into the ground at both
ends of the tent with the nails at a steep angle, as shown.
Nail the four corners of the sheet into the ground through
several thicknesses.

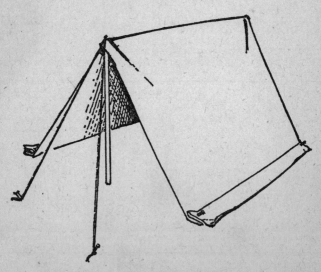

Rope Ladder

YOU WILL NEED
*Pieces of wood 25 mm × 6 cm
× 30 cm*
2 lengths of ½" nylon rope
Sandpaper
Wood preservative

SPECIAL EQUIPMENT
A drill with a 12 mm (½") bit

1 Drill two 12 mm (½") holes through each piece of wood, 30 mm from either end. Sandpaper each piece smooth.

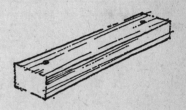

2 If your rope ladder is to stay out of doors, the wood must be painted all over with a wood preservative and left to dry.

3 Make double knots in the ends of the ropes and thread them through the holes in the first rung. Tie knots above each hole, then tie two more knots 25 cm (10") above these. Thread the next rung on to the ropes, make firm knots above that, and so on. When you have secured the last rung, leave plenty of rope above it for tying the ladder in place.

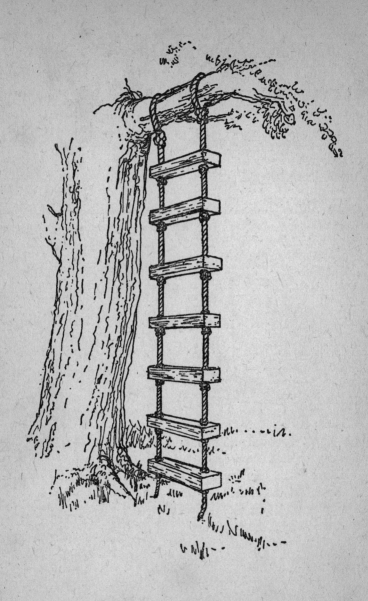

4 When attaching your rope ladder to a tree, it is essential that you get a grown-up to help you fix it safely.

Boozaphone

YOU WILL NEED
A length of broomhandle or
  25 mm (1") sq. wood
2 chairs
String
A number of bottles
A wooden spoon

SPECIAL EQUIPMENT
None

1 Tie the length of wood firmly to the backs of the chairs.

2 Fill the bottles with varying amounts of water and hang them from the crosspiece – far enough apart so that they do not hit each other when they swing. The fuller they are, the higher the note they will give when struck.

Using a wooden spoon as a striker, experiment with the levels of water in the bottles until you can play a tune on them.

113

Magnetic Theatre

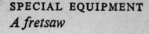

YOU WILL NEED

4 *pieces of* 40 cm (16″) *square hardboard*
80 cm (32″) *length of 3 cm (1¼″) square wood*
About 2 metres of battening
Several sheets of strong card
Wood glue
Small, semi-circular magnets
Dowelling to fit into the magnets
Metal washers
Scraps of balsa wood

SPECIAL EQUIPMENT
A fretsaw

1 Cut the length of wood in half and glue the pieces between two squares of hardboard, as shown, to form the stage.

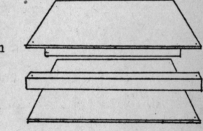

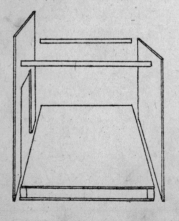

2 Cut 5 cm off one side of the third piece of hardboard, and, using a fretsaw, cut a rectangular hole in the last piece. Cut two 40 cm lengths of battening and assemble the four pieces as shown. Then nail or glue them firmly to each other and to the stage.

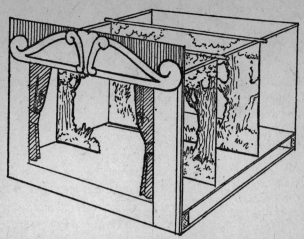

3 Make and paint cut-out scenery from card, glue each piece to a length of battening and hang it across the stage. Paint a backdrop on card and glue it to the back of the theatre. Paint the front of the theatre with pillars or curtains.

4 Make painted cut-out characters approximately 12 cm high, from stiff card, and fix them into slots cut into small balsa blocks. (You could also use plastic model figures.) Glue a metal washer under each character.

5 Cut 45 cm lengths of dowelling and glue them firmly into the magnets. Stand your characters on the stage, connect each one with a magnet pushed underneath the stage – and you're ready to operate your magnetic theatre.

Code Disc

YOU WILL NEED
Thick paper or card
Split-pin paper fasteners – or
upholstery tacks and a cork

SPECIAL EQUIPMENT
Protractor and compass

Here is a foolproof way of sending secret messages in code which can only be translated by possessors of this simple-to-make code disc. You will need to make more than one.

1 Draw two circles on to the card, one with a radius 10 mm smaller than the other. Then draw another circle inside each one, 10 mm from the outside edge.

2 With a protractor, mark off 36 points, 10° apart, round each outside circle. Rule a line from each point to the centre. In the 36 boxes round the edge of each circle, write the letters of the alphabet and the numbers 1 – 10.

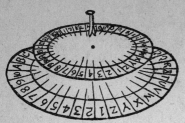

3 Cut out the two discs. With the smaller one on top, fix a paper fastener through both centres so that the top disc will revolve. (Or stick an upholstery nail through both centres into a piece of cork.)

4 Now you are ready to begin sending secret messages. First, choose any letter, or number, as the key to your code. Find it on the top disc, and revolve that disc so that the key letter is opposite A on the bottom disc. Start your message by writing your code key. Here it is **AZ** (or, to confuse the enemy even more, it can be called **B1**, or **C2**, and so on). Keeping the discs in the **AZ** position, spell out your message by finding the correct letters on the bottom disc, but writing down the letters that appear opposite them on the top disc. To put would-be infiltrators off the scent even more, don't leave any gaps between the coded words.

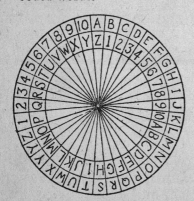

(The message reads, "Secret meeting tonight 5.15".)

117

Shadow Show

YOU WILL NEED
A white sheet
Some bright lights
A table and cloth
Card
Thin dowelling or plant sticks
Newspaper

SPECIAL EQUIPMENT
None

1 Pin the sheet up across a doorway, making it as taut as possible. Put a table covered with a cloth in front of it.

2 Cut out characters from card and attach a stick or piece of dowelling to the back of each with Sellotape, giving you a handle at least 15 cm (6″) long.

3 Make scenery out of newspaper, through which a certain amount of light will shine, and tape it to the back of the sheet.

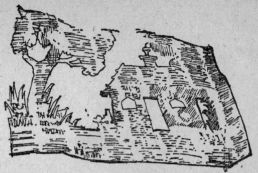

4 Shine one or more bright lights on to the sheet from behind, and operate your cut-outs from below table level.

The shadow show will work best when the audience is in complete darkness, and no light escapes round the sides of the sheet. Hold your characters as flat as possible against the sheet, and make sure that no parts of yourself can be seen in silhouette too.

Clock Golf

YOU WILL NEED
A small flowerpot
12 small plywood squares
12 15 cm (6″) nails
Paint
A golf club and golf balls

SPECIAL EQUIPMENT
None

1 Paint the plywood squares with the numbers 1 to 12. Hammer a nail through the centre of each one.

2 Sink the flowerpot in the centre of your golf lawn. Starting with number 1, stick the squares into the ground in a clockwise circle around the pot, making each number a different distance from it.

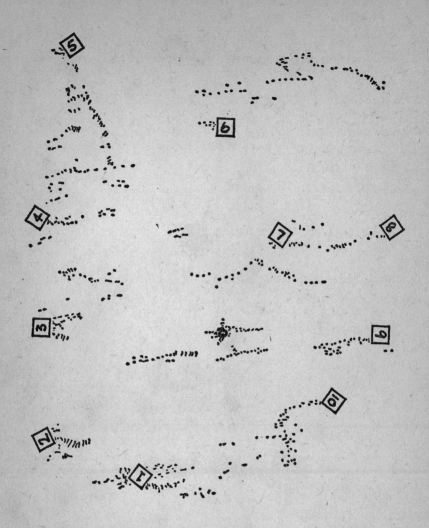

3 Taking it in turns to play a shot, each player starts at number 1, and sinks their ball in the pot from each number in turn. The first player to complete the course is the winner.

Make Your Own Presents

Hal Danby

The best presents are those you make yourself – and they're the most fun to give.

Here's an exciting book which launches Armada's new Hobbies and Leisure list. It's full of super ideas for presents to give all your family and friends. Most of them can be made easily and cheaply – often from odds and ends you can find around the house.

The step-by-step instructions are fully illustrated – and there are presents to make for everyone:

How about a hanging basket for Mum, a table lamp for Dad, or a topsy-turvey doll for a younger sister? You could make a woolly car stopper for the garage in an afternoon. Or what about a set of photograph drink coasters for Grandma?

(Or you could give the book as a present and hope someone makes one of these presents for you!)

Armada

The Trickster's Handbook
200 tricks, jokes and stunts to fool your friends

Peter Eldin

Instant Magic!
Astonish your friends in 200 hilarious ways.
Prove that 19 equals 20 . . . tear a telephone directory
in half . . . tell fortunes with a banana . . . float a
sausage in mid-air . . .

How's it done? Only you know, when you've got a copy
of The Trickster's Handbook. So keep it in a secret
place while you baffle your victims with fiendish stunts
and leg-pulls.

Another exciting Fun Book from Armada

Armada

The Secret Agent's Handbook
A guide for sleuths, spies and private eyes

Peter Eldin

Warning!
Before opening this book, make sure the coast is clear.
Inside you will find Top Secret Information. Be careful –
it must not fall into the wrong hands. (And you never
know where enemy agents may be lurking.)

Here's the low-down on ... Coded Messages ... Secret
Handshakes ... Disguises ... Passwords ... Spy
Traps ... Agents' Language ... Invisible Writing ...
The Toothpaste Hideout ... and many more highly
confidential instructions on how to become a Top
Secret Agent.

Top Priority
If you are captured with this handbook in your
possession – swallow it!

Another exciting Fun Book from Armada

Armada

CAPTAIN ARMADA

has a whole shipload of exciting books for you

Here are just some of the best-selling titles that Armada has to offer:

☒ **Make Your Own Presents** Hal Danby 75p

☒ **The Trickster's Handbook** Peter Eldin 50p

☒ **The Secret Agent's Handbook** Peter Eldin 65p

☒ **Fun on Wheels** Mary Danby 50p

☒ **Armada Quiz and Puzzle Book No. 4**
Doris Dickens & Mary Danby 50p

☒ **The 2nd Armada Book of Cartoons** Mary Danby 40p

☒ **Sports Quiz Book** Gordon Jeffery 60p

☒ **The 2nd Armada Book of Fun** Mary Danby 40p

☒ **Fun to Know About Dogs** Michele Brown 60p

☒ **The New Armada TV Quiz Book** Peter Eldin 50p

Armadas are available in bookshops and newsagents, but can also be ordered by post.

HOW TO ORDER
ARMADA BOOKS, Cash Sales Dept., GPO Box 29, Douglas, Isle of Man, British Isles. Please send purchase price of book plus postage, as follows:—

    1—4 Books .... 8p per copy
    5 Books or more .... no further charge
    25 Books sent post free within U.K.

Overseas Customers
    1 Book: 10p. Additional books 5p per copy

NAME (Block letters)

ADDRESS